Love Poems

of

Arif Khudairi

Copyright © October 2011
All rights reserved.

This publication may not be reproduced, in whole or in part, by any means including photocopying or any information storage or retrieval system, without the specific and prior written permission of the author and publisher.

This book is sold subject to the condition that it shall not, by way of trade or otherwise, be re-sold, hired out, or otherwise circulated without the author's or publisher's prior consent in any form of binding or cover other than that in which it is published and without a similar condition including this condition being imposed on the subsequent purchaser.

First Edition: October 2011
Published by Nsemia Inc. Publishers (www.nsemia.com)

Edited By: Charles Phebih-Agyekum
Cover Concept & Illustration: Arif Khudairi
Cover Design: Danielle Pitt
Layout Design: Kemunto Matunda

Note for Librarians:
A cataloguing record for this book is available from Library and Archives Canada.

ISBN: 978-1-926906-11-9

For Mai

By the Same Poet

Trees Leaves (anthology)
The Rubaiyat of Arif Khudairi (anthology)
Abode of Peace (anthology)
Tales From the Arabian Sahara (short stories)
Tales of the Prophets (short stories)
The Eighth Voyage of Sinbad (novella)

Contents

By The Same Poet ii
About The Author..v
Foreword..vii
Introduction..ix
The Mirror..1
In The Shade of Your Eyelashes 3
For Your Eyes...5
Wish...7
That Was All..9
Love..11
Your Love..13
I Love You...15
True Love..17
Love Poem..19
My Love Poems...21
A Love Poem About You....................................23
Love Song...25
Every Time I Write...27
The Language of Love.......................................29
Like You..30
The Flower of Flowers.......................................32
I Know..34
Because You Are...36
Without You..38
Your City...40
Life..42
How Can I Forget You..44
Beautiful Dream...46
I Will Survive...47
Set Me Free..49
Did I Tell You...50
Thinking of You...52
Black Coffee...54
Love Knows No Season....................................56
Doves of Light..58
Birthday Present...60
How I Feel About You.......................................62
When You Come..64
The Temple of Love..67
The Poems..70
You Live Within Me...71
Within My Heart..73
Everywhere..74
The Flower..75

About the Author

A prolific and bilingual writer in English and Arabic, Dr Arif Karkhi Abukhudairi has published 47 books including essays, collections of short stories, folk tales, poems and translations. His fourteen volumes of poetry include *Trees Leaves* (Pentland, 1998), *Rubaiyat of Arif Khudairi* (al-Hadarah al-Arabia, 2004) and *Abode of Peace* (DBP, 2008). His short stories collection, *Tales From the Arabian Sahara: The Trip and Other Stories*, was released in 1998 by Minerva Press, London and his novella, *The Eighth Voyage of Sinbad*, came out in 1999 at the same press. In 2010, this book was translated into Arabic and published in Cairo (General Egyptian Book Organization). His work has appeared in publications in Egypt, Malaysia, Oman, Yemen, India, Pakistan, UK, Canada, Indonesia, Brunei, Colombia and USA. Some of his poems have been anthologized in *Theatre of the Mind, Under the Canopy and Other Poems*, in 1999 and elsewhere. He is a guest poet in several international poetry festivals including Brunei international poetry reading (1994) and the XX International Poetry festival in Medellin, Colombia (2010).

He is the founder and editor of *The Journal of Arabic Studies*, as well as president of the Poetry Society, University of Brunei Darussalam. He was named Poet of the Month by three American journals in 2000, 2001, 2004 and 2005 and received several Poetry Awards. He has translated seven books of poems from Korean, Malay, Persian, and English into Arabic. His work has been translated into Arabic, English, Spanish, Malay, Bahasa Indonesia and Urdu. In 1995, 2005 and 2010, he was listed in *Who's Who in Translation and Terminology*, *The International Who's Who in Poetry*, and *Antologia Poesia Universal*, respectively.

Arif holds a Ph.D. in Arabic literature from Cairo University and has held teaching posts at several universities, including the University of Wisconsin, Madison, Hankuk University for Foreign Studies, Seoul, and the National University of Malaysia. He is an associate professor at the Sultan Sharif Ali Islamic University, Brunei Darussalam where he teaches research methodology, theories of translation and comparative literature and was formerly the Dean of Faculty of Arabic Language and Islamic Civilization at Sultan Sharif Ali Islamic University of Brunei Darussalam. He is also a member of the Academy of Modern Arabic Literature, and the Egyptian Writers Association in Cairo, Egypt.

FOREWORD

Those who have been lucky enough to have been in love will marvel at the poems within these pages and at how Arif has found or created new words to describe these magical feelings... for you who await...Arif may well whet your appetite.

Through the pages of this magical, mystical wonderland, we are allowed to watch and experience feelings be they gentle, stunning, thought provoking, poignant...the merry and misery go rounds of love. We peep through the door or over their shoulders at the early floundering and questioning as they get deeper and more deeply entwined.

He slips easily onto his boat to cross the seven seas and moments later we are mesmerized when more pages away we find the joys and beauties of ancient Egypt. It is very tempting to quote phrase after beautiful phrase, but I will leave it to the fair reader to discover these treasures written by a fine modern troubadour.

Sylvia Lukeman,
President,
Poets Who Care,
Liverpool, England.

Introduction

Love Poems of Arif Khudairi
By Professor S.R. Siddiqui
Karachi, Pakistan

Arif Khudairi is not only a poet, but a Philosopher-Poet. He is a learned and well-read scholar. He studied widely and at last he stands in the long line of the well-known poets of the east, starting from Hafiz, Omar Khayyam, Rumi and ending with Iqbal.

The metaphysical philosophy of these great poets of the east is not a simple one. It is nevertheless one of the greatest philosophies of all mankind. The theme of that metaphysical theory, very simply, is that the whole Universe, with each and every thing therein, is a reflection of the Magnanimity of its Master. It is only a shadow of its Creator and a mirror in which the beauty of the Supreme Authority can be seen. Man's role in the Universe is pivotal in so far as he finds himself endlessly inspired to praise the beauty and magnificence he sees in such abundance around him. He looks in wonder at the beauty of the stars in the night and the beauty of flowers in the garden and he is compelled to praise them. Nevertheless, when he praises the beauty around him, he is in fact praising its Creator.

Arif Khudairi is a skilful artist. He is rendering that metaphysical theory in his poems. He is transferring that eastern thought to the west. He has such a marvellous command over the subject that one cannot easily perceive the theme lying beneath his poetry unless one takes time to grasp its real meaning.

He expressed himself fully in his poem "You Live Within Me". It is a superb poem and a masterpiece of its kind. It resounds like the words of the great eastern mystic poets such as Hafiz and Rumi. They always express the thought that the whole Universe and everything therein is like a shadow or a mirror of the Magnificence of the Creator and, as man has a unique existence within it, he always seeks His pleasure and loves Him to the core of his heart. Khudairi says: "In spite/ Of the rivers/ Of the seas/ Of the oceans/ That separate the two of us/ You still live/ Within me." He feels the love of his Creator in his heart, mind and soul. This divine love goes on and runs deep within him: "You continue/ To run/ In my blood."

Each and everything in this world has no real existence. It is a temporary and borrowed existence that will soon perish. The life of man in this world has no reality. It is deceptive and flows through time. Khudairi says: "Life is/ A dream/ Only a day/ Or two/ We come here/ One day/ And one day/ We go/ We know not/ Why we come/ Nor why/ We leave."

Love, however, which is the most precious and the most beautiful feeling in the world, does not fade away like other mortal things. It is as old as this world and it shall remain forever. The poet says: "My love/ For you/ Is as old/ As the sun/ As the stars/ And the moon/ It has been/ Always there/ Like the heavens/ And the earth/ It has been/ Always flowing/ Like the river/ And the sea."

This tender and aesthetic feeling in man remains hidden in one's own self and suddenly appears without prior notice. Let us hear from the poet: "No one had/ Told me/ Anything/ About love/ At the time/ I was young/ Love to me/ Was a true/ Tender feeling/ As beautiful/ As a dream."

Love Poems of Arif Khudairi is indeed a marvellous collection. Its profound and lively poems arouse the aesthetic sense within its reader. The melody of the poetry is high and the construction is precise. It is an anthology that will definitely take its place among the works of the great love poets.

Arif Khudairi

The Mirror

Blessed you are
My beloved,
And blessed
Are your body,
And your soul
Together.
For in you,
You gather
The mines of earth,
And the treasures,
Of heavens.
You possess
The nights
And the dawns,
The brooks,
And the woods,
And the fruits.
Every time
I look at you,
I see
An orchard
Of charm,
A meadow
Of elegance,
A garden
Of grace.
I see
A river
Of bliss,
A cascade
Of gold,
A sea
Of light.

I see
A swan
And a gazelle,
A mare,
And a camel,
A mermaid
And a houri.
And like
A mirror of magic,
You reflect
All beauties
On earth,
And in heavens,
In meadows
And rivers,
In forests
And seas.

Arif Khudairi

In The Shade of Your Eyelashes

At sunrise,
Your eyes
Are two streams
Of amber,
Two doves
In love,
Two melodies
Of longing,
Of magic,
Of affection.
For whom,
For whom,
Do they sing
Their love songs,
At sunrise?

At sunset,
Your eyes
Are two islands
Of oranges,
Of rainbow,
Of tulips.
For whom,
For whom,
Do they shed
Their smiles,
When the sun
Goes down?

At night,
Your eyes
Are two stars
Full of rapture,
Of charm,

Of wine.
May I,
May I,
Spend the night
In the shade
Of your long
Eyelashes?

At sunrise,
At sunset,
And at night,
I write
My love poems,
About you,
With a smile,
As my eyes
Dream of
Your eyes.

Bandar Seri Begawan,
2001

For Your Eyes

For your eyes,
My deep,
Mystery seas,
And blue,
Wide skies,
I defied
All the world,
I fought
All the chieftains
Of the tribes.
I competed
With them,
And I won
All my fights.
I met
All the challenges
With a smile.
I accepted
The conditions
You laid
Down for
The lovers
Of your eyes.
I climbed
The lofty hills,
I walked
Through the deserts,
I flew
In the skies.
I crossed
The seven seas
I travelled
To the far,

Fairy islands,
And brought
In my boat
Rare diamonds,
Pure amber,
Lotus flowers,
And tulips,
Red,
Purple,
And white,
And spread
All of them
At your feet
As a token
Of my love
For you,
And for
The sake
Of your eyes.

Wish

When I look
Into the heavens
In your eyes,
I realize
That you are
Much prettier
Than the moon.
In your eyes,
I can see
The moonlight,
The sunrise,
And the colour
Of the river.
When I look
Into the heavens
In your eyes,
I wish
I were
King Solomon,
With his gold,
With his power,
With his jinn.
For you,
I would build
A lofty palace
Of diamonds,
I would fetch
Red tulips,
Pure amber,
And rare
Precious emeralds.
I would give you
Everything

You would wish.
For when
I look
Into the heavens
In your eyes,
I realize
That with you
I will dream,
Like a child,
Day and night.
I will write
A thousand poems
About you,
And about
Your eyes.

That Was All

Like a moon,
You looked
At me,
And smiled.
That was all.
And I,
Ever since,
Have nothing
On my mind
Save your face,
Your lips,
And your eyes.
You only
Looked at me,
And smiled.
That was all.
Then you quietly,
Walked away
As though
Nothing happened,
Though you set
My chest
Ablaze.
You drove
Me mad
With your love,
As *Laila*
Once did
To *Majnun*.
And now,
You sleep
Like a child,
And smile

In your dreams,
While I
Stay awake
All the nights
Thinking of
Your face,
Your lips,
And your eyes.

Love

It is love
When you cannot
Express
What you feel
For someone,
When your words
Make no sense,
When you want
To be
With the beloved
All the time,
When you stay
Always awake
The whole night,
When you look
At the moon,
And talk
To the stars,
When you hope,
When you fear,
When you frown,
When you smile,
When a flower
Is presented
In affection,
With a smile,
When you feel,
Sometimes,
As if you live
In hell,
And sometimes
In paradise.
It is love

When you sigh,
When you long,
When you feel
As if you see
The whole life
Looks new
In your eyes.
It is love
That makes
You love
The abode
Of the beloved
And love
Your life.
Without love
You cannot
Pretend
You are
Really alive.

Your Love

Your love,
My love,
Taught me
Many things
About life,
And about
You and me,
Taught me
How to read
The language
Of your eyes,
And the signs
Of your lips,
Taught me
How to dream
At day,
How to wake
At night,
Taught me that
Love is
A gift,
A blessing,
A power
That makes
Us endure
The hardships
Of our life,
And that
With love,
Life looks
Prettier than
Paradise.
Your love,

My love,
Taught me much,
Taught me
Wonderful things.
Yet in spite
Of what
Your love
Has taught me,
I still
Do not know
Many things
About love,
And many things
About you.

I Love You

I love you
For your eyes
Make me
Love the seas,
The rivers,
And the skies,
And dream
About you
All the time.

I love you
For your lips
Make me
Love the roses,
The flowers,
And the tulips
And fly
In the sky
As a drunken
Butterfly.

I love you
For your smile
Makes me
Love the sun,
The moon,
And the stars,
And wait
For the dawn
Every day
In delight.

I love you
For you
Make me
Love the birds,
The streams,
And the trees,
And swim
In a river
Made of musk,
Of charm,
And dream.

Arif Khudairi

True Love

It is true
I love you,
Sweetheart,
Not because
You have
A pretty face
With wide
Blue eyes
Like the color
Of the skies,
And delicious
Sultry lips
Made of soft,
Red tulips.
I love you,
My beloved,
Not for
The music
In your voice
Which falls,
From your lips
Like sweet,
Ripe peaches.
Nor for
Your breasts,
Your waist,
Nor your elegant
Long neck
Like a swan.
I love you,
My darling,
Not for this
Nor for that;

For this
Kind of love
Is not
A real love.
I love you,
Dearest one,
For what
I can see
With the eye
Of my heart
Deep within
Your skin,
And beyond
The colour
And the size
Of your eyes,
And your lips.
I love you,
My love,
For the sake
Of love,
And for you.

Arif Khudairi

Love Poem

Everyday,
When I open
My eyes,
And see
Sunrise,
I see you,
And your eyes,
And long
To write
A love poem
That depicts
What I feel
About you,
And about
Your eyes.
A love poem
That flows,
Like a river,
From my heart
To your heart.
Not a poem
That may dazzle
Your eyes
With mere rhetoric,
Word play,
And rhyme.
Nor a poem
That looks
Like the poems
That love poets
Usually write.
Everyday,
When I open

My eyes,
And see
Sunrise,
I see you,
And your eyes,
And long
To write
A love poem,
A true poem,
A simple poem
That depicts
What I feel
About you,
And about
Your eyes.

My Love Poems

You ask,
As they ask,
Time and again,
Who is she,
The woman
For whom
I write
My love poems?
Is she tawny?
Is she blonde?
Does she have
Blue eyes?
Or black?
Or brown?
You ask,
As they ask,
Time and again,
Who is she,
My love?
Is she
An angel
In my mind?
Or real
Like me?
You ask,
As they do,
Everyday.
Though if
You just
Look into
My heart,
You will see
Your face,

Your eyes,
Your lips,
As if
You look
Into a mirror.
You will know
That the woman
For whom
I write
My love poems
Is no one
Other than
You yourself:
My poem,
My flower,
And the love
That fills
My life
With delight,
With rapture,
And pride.

Arif Khudairi

A Love Poem About You

Forgive me,
My love,
If I
Couldn't write
A love poem
About you,
And about
Your eyes.
For how
Can I write
Love poems
In this
Strange age,
In which
Poetry has
No place,
And people
Are no longer
Interested
In romance,
And in rhyme?

Forgive me,
My love,
If I
Couldn't write
A love poem
About you,
And about
Your lips,
When children
Starve to death
At day,
And at night.

Forgive me,
My love,
If I
Couldn't write
A love poem
About you,
And about
Your hair,
In a world
Where words
Lost their meanings,
Their effects.

Forgive me,
My love,
If I
Couldn't write
A love poem
About you,
And about
Your eyes,
Your lips,
And your hair.
Forgive me,
Forgive me.

Bandar Seri Begawan,
29/3/2002

Arif Khudairi

Love Song

Do not cry,
My love,
When I die.
Instead,
Wear the smile
That I love
To see
On your lips,
And come
To my tomb,
And recite
A love poem.
I will smile
In my grave,
In satisfaction,
In delight,
In content.
For you know,
I, always,
Love to sing
Love songs.
I cannot
Bear to see
Tears in
The eyes
That I love
More than life.
And I wish
To live
A hundred years,
But alas!
I cannot.
Instead,

Now, I wish
To live
In my poems
As long
As lovers
Read them
To their dearest,
Loved ones.
I will, then,
Think of you,
Of the smile
That I love
To see
On your lips,
And smile
In my grave,
In satisfaction,
In delight,
In content.

Arif Khudairi

Every Time I Write

Every time,
I sit down
To write
A love poem
For you,
My love,
I wonder
How can language
Ever capture
The essence
Of your beauty?
How can language
Paint the depth
Of your eyes,
And the rays
Of your smile?
How can language
Describe
The emotions
Deep inside,
And show
You exactly
How I feel
About you?
Every time,
I sit down
To write
A love poem
For you,
My love,
I wonder,
And realize
That your charm

Is, simply,
Beyond the language
And above
All the words
And the style.
Yet, I write
In my poor,
Simple language,
Using shallow,
Humble words;
For writing
My love poems
For you,
My love,
Makes my life
Worthy to live,
Adds to it
A new meaning
And provides
Me with
A purpose,
A vision,
A delight.

Arif Khudairi

The Language of Love

Because we
Are in love,
We say not:
You and I.
For I melted
In you and,
You melted
In me.

Because we
Are in love,
Hence we
Say we.
For we now
Are one,
Not two.
We are we.

Because we
Are in love,
You are me.
I am you.
With my heart,
You feel now.
With your eyes,
I now see.

Because we
Are in love,
We say not:
You and I.
For I melted
In you and,
You melted
In me.

Bandar Seri Begawan,
18/9/2002

Like You

Let me
Tell you
I love you
To see
The moonlight
Beam tenderly
In the skies
Of your eyes,
And to view
The sun rise
Within the islands
Of your lips.
Let me
Tell you
I love you
To hear
The melodies
In the waves
Of your voice.
Let me
Tell you
I love you
To refine
My words,
To refresh
My images,
To make
My feelings
More tender.
Let me
Tell you
I love you
To renew

Arif Khudairi

My blood,
To become
A bit younger,
And to be
Reborn
Anew.
Let me
Tell you
I love you
To make life
Look prettier.
To teach
The nightingales
How to sing,
And to fill
Our world
With love poems,
More tender,
More inspiring,
More beautiful,
Like you.

The Flower of Flowers

In my eyes,
And in
My heart,
You look
Like the flower
Of flowers.
No girl in
This life
Can compete
With you,
In your charm:
With your silky,
Golden hair
As long
As night,
With your sweet,
Delicious lips
Made of soft,
Red tulips,
With your blue,
Wide eyes
Like clear,
Smiling skies,
With your melodic,
Gentle steps
When you walk,
And I look
At your looks,
In affection,
In longing,
In delight,
Till you finally,
Like a soft,

Arif Khudairi

Snow cloud,
Melt quickly
In the crowd,
And leave
Me dreaming
Of hair
Like spikes,
Of lips
Like tulips,
Of eyes
Like blue,
Wide skies.

I Know

I know,
My dear,
A minute ago
You were here.
But now,
I miss you.
And here
Everything
Reminds me
Of you:
Your flowers,
Your perfume,
Your umbrella,
Your magazine.
And when
I close
My eyes,
I see you
Slip gently
In your bed,
And soon,
Fall in
A river
Of dreams.
And when
I open
My eyes,
I look
At the sky,
And see
The moon,
Like you,
Swims in

Arif Khudairi

Rosy dreams.
I smile,
And wait
For sunrise
As I write
A love poem
About you.

Because You Are

Because you are
The true friend
Whom I
Can find
At my side
Day or night.
Because you make
My long,
Wintry nights
Romantically warm,
And bright.
Because you are
The oak tree
In whose shade
I sit
And rest
In the hot,
Summer days.
Because you fill
My life
With your charm,
With your laughter,
With your bright,
Sunny smile.
Because you make
Life look
More beautiful
In my eyes.
Because you are
So beautiful,
So loveable,
So humble.
Because you

Arif Khudairi

Do not lie,
And do not
Pretend.
Because you are
My dream,
And reality.
Because you are
Who you are,
I love you
Respect you,
And want
To live
With you
Till the end
Of my life.

Without You

Sometimes,
At day,
And sometimes,
At night,
I sit
By myself,
And wonder:
What my life
Would be
Without you
And without
The joy,
And the light
You brought
To my life.
Then I sigh
In relief,
In content,
In satisfaction,
And smile.
For I was
So lonely,
So blue,
So down
Before I set
My eyes
Upon your magical,
Blue eyes,
Your shining,
Dawn-like,
Peaceful smile,
Your thousand
And one

Wonders that
Make me,
Sometimes,
Sit down
By myself
At day,
And sometimes,
At night,
And wonder:
What my life
Would be
Without you?
Then I sigh
In rapture,
In content,
In gratitude
And smile.

Your City

Yesterday,
In your city,
Sweetheart,
I saw
Many things,
Beautiful things,
Amazing things:
I saw rivers,
And hills.
I saw gardens
As beautiful
As paradise,
And skies
Like lakes
Full of light.
I saw palaces,
Yellow,
Red,
And white.
I saw roses
Smiling like
Moonlight.

Yesterday,
In your city,
Sweetheart,
I saw
Many things,
Beautiful things,
Amazing things.
Yet when
I left,
I forgot

Arif Khudairi

The rivers,
The palaces,
And the skies.
I forgot
The pretty faces
Of the maidens
Like dawn.
I forgot
Everything
Save your face,
Your smile,
And sweet,
Tender memories
Like a scented
Night breeze
Blowing gently
Through the trees.

Life

Life is
A dream.
Only a day,
Or two.
We come here
One day,
And one day,
We go.
We know not
Why we come,
Nor why
We leave.
And you,
My sweet,
Are simply
All I need
In this life.
I love you,
And you
Love me.
Why then
Do we waste
Our time
In separation?
Your stunning,
Precious beauty
Will fade
Like a flower,
And you
Will regret
That you
Had not
Enjoyed

Arif Khudairi

Your life
As you should.
Come love,
Let's live
Together,
For a while,
Before dawn
Knocks on
Our door,
And awakes
Us from
Our dream.

How Can I Forget You

People say,
Time can
Heal the wounds,
By and by,
And erase
The agony,
The sorrow,
And the pain.
People say,
To forget
A woman,
You may love
A new woman.
And I
Have tried
Everything
That I could.
But I failed
To forget
About you,
And about
Your love.
And now,
I see you
Everywhere
I go:
I see you
In the flowers,
In the birds,
And the trees.
I see you
In the sun,
At day,

And the moon,
At night.
I see you
In the women
I encounter
On the lonely,
Long road
Of my life.
Tell me, please:
How can I
Forget you?
How can I
Take off
Your love?
How can I
Live my life
Without you?

Beautiful Dream

No one had
Told me
Anything
About love.
At the time,
I was young.
Love to me
Was a true,
Tender feeling,
As beautiful
As a dream.
And when
You told me
You loved me,
And your love
For me
Would last
Forever,
I believed
What you said.
For I
Was young,
And a dreamer.
Even now,
I have not
Changed much.
I still
See love
As I used
To see it
Yesterday:
A true,
Genuine and
Tender feeling
As beautiful
As a dream.

Arif Khudairi

I Will Survive

The night
Is long,
And lonely.
You are not
Now around.
Yesterday,
I thought
If you would
Leave me,
Life would
Leave me
As well.
The sky
Would shed,
Her tears,
Day and night.
The stars
Would vanish
From the heavens,
And the moon
Would never
Smile again.
I thought
If you would
Leave me,
The world
Would come
To an end.
And I would
Not survive.
That was
What I thought
Until
You left.

Yet life is
Still around.
The eyes
Of the skies
Are not wet.
The stars
Have not left.
And the moon
Has not lost
Her smile.
You left,
And the night
Is long,
And lonely.
Yet I
Will l survive.

Arif Khudairi

Set Me Free

If you
Love me,
Set me free.
Love is not
A command,
Neither is it
A possession.
Love is
A flower
That requires
Raindrops,
Fresh air,
Sunshine,
A bird
That needs
To fly,
In the sky,
Not to stay
In a cage,
Or a tree.
You cannot
Tie me
To your looks.
You cannot
Buy me
With your wealth.
If you
Love me,
Set me free.
For love comes
When we both
Are free.

Bandar Seri Begawan,
13/12/2001

Did I Tell You

The light
Fills the night
With delight.
And you are
Like a flower,
A princess,
A houri.
May I have
This dance?
May I hold
Your hand,
The whole night?

Did I tell you
You are beautiful?
But you know.
You hear it
In the whispers
Of the breeze,
And the sighs
Of women.
You see it
In your mirror,
And the eyes
Of men.

Did I tell you
I love you?
Yes, perhaps,
I did
A thousand times.
Let me then,
Say it again,

Arif Khudairi

And again,
And again,
With my lips,
With my touch,
With my eyes.

Did I tell you
You dance well?
And I wish
The dance,
And the night,
Never stop.
Did I
Tell you
You are beautiful?
Did I
Tell you
I love you?

Bandar Seri Begawan,
22/2/2002

Thinking of You

When I sit
At sunset
In my garden,
And think
Of the days
Of my life
Which flew
Like wind,
I recall
All the battles
That I fought,
And lost,
And the ships
In which
I crossed
The seven seas,
And returned
To my land,
Empty handed:
With no lamps,
With no carpets,
With no rings,
I recall,
As well,
All the sorrows,
All the pains,
And all
The despairs,
And shake
My head,
In regret.
Then I think
Of you:

Arif Khudairi

Your face,
Your eyes,
Your lips,
And at once,
All the sorrows,
All the pains,
And all
The despairs,
Disappear,
And I smile,
In satisfaction,
In admiration,
In content.
Bandar Seri Begawan,
27/5/2002

Black Coffee

We have not
Talked much lately.
Neither have
Our eyes.
We do not
Hold hands.
We do not
Now smile.
This café is
A bit cold.
Don't you think?
What do you like
To drink?
I will have
Black coffee.
How're you
Doing lately?
Mignon, my dog,
Is a bit depressed.
Nothing is new.
Only children
Starve to death.
Are you seeing someone?
Drink, drink.
Your coffee
Is getting cold.
This Café is
A bit cold.
Don't you think?
It is raining outside.
Winter is
Not my favorite.
Do you want
Some more coffee?

Arif Khudairi

I do not know why
I think
Of Brasilia
Right now.
Is there
A new thing
In your life?
I have not
Written much poetry
These days.
We have not
Talked much lately.
Neither have
Our eyes,
Nor our hands.
Drink your coffee.
Drink your coffee.

Bandar Seri Begawan,
3/10/2002

Love Knows No Season

I love you.
You love me.
I know that
For sure.
I can see it
In your eyes.
So why
Do you try
To conceal
What you feel
For me?
Because
You are
Autumn, and
I am
Spring,
And there are
So many winters
Between you
And me?
Maybe.
But love
Knows
No season.
People love
In autumn
As they do
In spring.
My dawn seeks
Your night,
My flowers
Long for
Your rain,

Arif Khudairi

And my sun
Shines when
My eyes
Meet your eyes.
With you,
I feel
More beautiful,
More precious,
More secure.
I love you,
You love me.
So why
Do you conceal
What you feel
For me?

Bandar Seri Begawan
2006

Doves of Light

Sweetheart,
With your hair,
With your eyes,
With your lips,
You reflect
All the beauties
In the forests,
And the heavens,
And the seas.
In your hair
I see
Cataract,
Waves,
Colour of night,
In your eyes
I see
Violets,
Lakes,
Wide skies.
In your lips
I see
Red tulips,
Strawberries,
Daybreak light.
In your chest
I see
pomegranates,
Grapes,
Doves of light.
Sweetheart,
About you,

Arif Khudairi

And about
Your hair,
Your eyes,
Your lips,
Your chest,
I dream
Day and night.

Bandar Seri Begawan
2006

Birthday Present

What should I
Offer you
On your
Birthday,
Sweetheart?
A flower?
But flowers
Quietly wither
In no time.

What should I
Offer you
On your
Birthday,
Sweetheart?
A necklace
Made of stars?
But stars
Disappear
At day.

What should I
Offer you
On your
Birthday,
Sweetheart?
A scarf
Made of sun?
But sun sets
At night.

What should I
Offer you

Arif Khudairi

On your
Birthday,
Sweetheart?
I should offer
You a poem
Of mine,
For it will
Remain
Forever
To tell
The flowers,
And the stars,
And the sun
About you,
Your beauty,
And my love
Four you.

Bandar Seri Begawan
2006

How I Feel About You

How do
I feel
About you,
Sweetheart?
I wish
I could
Tell you.
But how
Could I count
The stars
Of the skies,
Or the waves
Of the rivers,
And the seas,
Even if
I had
All the trees
As pens,
And the seas
As ink?
How could I
Have the words
That no one
Ever used
Before me?
How can I
Describe
A feeling
As wide
And profound
As your eyes,
As beautiful
And sweet

As the smile
Upon your lips?
How can I
Tell you,
Sweetheart,
How I feel
About you?

Bandar Seri Begawan
2005

When You Come

When you come,
I will make
The night,
That we will
Spend together,
The night
Of the nights.
I will cast
Pieces of
My smile,
To shed light,
As the stars.
And I will
Hang my heart,
As the moon
Of the skies.

When you come,
I will scatter
Cherry flowers
On your path
To the gate
Of my garden.
I will make
My arms
A bridge
On which
You will cross
To my cottage.
I will make
My eyes
Candlelight
Of the night.

Arif Khudairi

When you come,
I will
Place you,
Like a king,
In the bed
Of my heart.
I will shower
Your body
With amber.
I will
Sprinkle
Jasmine petals
On your shoulders,
And pour
Red wine
On your feet.

When you come,
I will open
The gate
To my garden
And I will
Offer you
My apples,
And my grapes,
With delight.

When you come,
I will warm
Your night
With my body.
And I will
Cover you,
With my silky,
Long hair
Until
Sunrise.

When you come
I will be
Born anew.
I will be
A paradise.
I will be
Everything
That you like
To see
In me.

Bandar Seri Begawan
2002

The Temple of Love

Come, beloved.
But before
We enter
Our temple
Of love,
Let us first
Take off
Our sandals,
Our hats,
Our clothes.
Let us offer
Our flowers,
Our fruits,
Our bread,
To the hungry,
And to the poor.
Let us light
Our candles
For the night
Of the nights.

Come, beloved.
But before
We hold
Our hands,
And embrace
Each other,
Let us first
Kneel down,
And pray
To the beloved
Of the beloved.

Come, beloved.
But before
Our lips
Meet in
A sacred kiss,
Let us first
Sit down,
Side by side,
On the ground,
Next to
The candlelight,
And read
A love poem,
From the Zaboor,
From the Bible,
From the Quran.

Come, beloved.
But before
We drink
Our cup
Of red wine,
Let us first
Sing together,
Let us dance,
Let us whirl,
Like a drunken
Butterfly,
For a while.

Come, beloved.
But before
Our bodies
Melt and
Become one,
Let our souls

Arif Khudairi

Embrace.
Let us become
A love tree,
Bearing thousands
Of heavenly,
Passion fruits,
And offering
Its shade,
Its fruits,
Its wine,
To the lovers
Of mankind.

Bandar Seri Begawan
2002

The Poems

These poems that I write
For you, sweetheart,
May look like
The rays of the sun,
Or the drops of the rain,
Or the scent of the flowers.
They may sound,
As they come out,
As the waters spring out
Of the fountains,
Or the fruits fall down
From the trees,
Although they cause me
So much pain,
And because of them
I sleep not at night,
And I shed so many tears.
Yet, if they look
As pure as dawn,
As pretty as moon,
It is because I write them
For you,
And because they take some
Of the magic of your eyes,
And the sweetness of your lips.
And when I present them
To you,
I wish not for anything
In return.
For thinking, only thinking,
That you might read them
At day, or at night,
Makes a poet like me
Dance in joy
All his life.

Arif Khudairi

You Live Within Me

In spite
Of the rivers,
Of the seas,
Of the oceans,
That separate
The two of us,
You still live
Within me.
And though
I know
That I have
No hope
To see you
With my eyes
I still
Read you
As a poem
When I
Retreat
To my bed,
Every night.
For you
Continue
To dwell
In my eyes.
You continue
To run
In my blood.
You continue
To live
Within me,
In spite
Of the passage

Of time,
And the rivers,
And the oceans,
And the seas
That separate
You from me.

Within My Heart

For you,
My beloved,
I looked,
Day and night.
I wandered
In the wilderness.
I roamed
In the sahara.
I soared
In the heavens.
I swam
In the seas.
I talked
To the birds.
I spoke
With the flowers.
I combed
All the caves.
I searched
All the shrines.
At last,
I have found
That you are
Within my heart.

Bandar Seri Begawan,
16/10/2002

Everywhere

How could I
Forget you,
Sweetheart?
How could I?
You grow
In my soul,
And flourish
In my eyes.
I see you
When I wake
At dawn,
And when
I sleep
At night.
I see you
In the moon,
In the swan,
In the blooms.
I hear you
In the murmur
Of the river,
In the songs
Of the bulbul,
In the whispers
Of the breeze.
At day,
And at night,
You appear
Everywhere
Around me,
And you dwell
Within my eyes,
And my heart,
And my soul.

Bandar Seri Begawan
2006

Arif Khudairi

The Flower

My love for you,
My beloved,
Is as old
As the moon
And the sun,
As the rivers
And the seas.
You and I
Are like
The flower
And the scent,
The river
And the waves.
And like
A drunken
Butterfly,
I was thrown
Into the fire
Of your love.
And within
Its flames,
I became
A drop
In your waves
Which grew
As a white
Water lily
By your river.
Hence, people
Do not think
Of you
Without me,
Nor of me
Without you.
At day,
They see us
Together
As they see
The sun

And the rays
Of the sun.
And at night,
They see us
Together
As they see
The moon
And the light
Of the moon.

Bandar Seri Begawan
2006

www.ingramcontent.com/pod-product-compliance
Lightning Source LLC
Chambersburg PA
CBHW030055170426
43197CB00010B/1536